Welcome to Haki and the Rule of Law, where you will lea[rn]
States' legal system help create a peaceful and fair so[ciety]
world history have used the American justice system a[s]
States every citizen is treated with equality.

Merle Wilberding

B.A. St. Mary's University (Minnesota)

J.D. University of Notre Dame

LL.M. George Washington University

M.B.A. University of Dayton

M.L.I.S. University of Wisconsin - Milwaukee

Librarian Certificate - Oxford University (UK)

Admitted to Practice: District of Columbia, Iowa and Ohio, United States Supreme Court

It is important to understand the Rule of Law so that you are able to make sure that you and others are treated with fairness and are given the same basic rights. You will also learn how you can better serve your community. When you know your rights and responsibilities in our country, you will appreciate why President Abraham Lincoln said in his historic Gettysburg Address that our government is "of the people, by the people and for the people."

"Haki" is the African Swahili word for justice, fairness and what is right, and represents the true meaning behind the phrase "the Rule of Law."

I am excited to introduce you to Haki, our mascot, who will be leading you through this book. Join Haki as he takes you on an exciting adventure through the Rule of Law and as he challenges you with fun learning activities to illustrate the Rule of Law.

I want to express our gratitude to the Ohio State Bar Foundation for its financial support for the updating, printing and distribution of this edition of Haki and the Rule of Law. I also want to thank Chris Stewart and the Dayton Daily News for their permission to use the above photograph.

Merle Wilberding

Merle Wilberding
Attorney At Law

The Rule Of Law

Throughout history people have tried to create a system of rules or laws that regulate and maintain specific ways for people to act: ways which are fair, respectful and preserve the well-being of others. For example, it is "fair, respectful and preserves the well-being of others" to honor other people's property, whether it is a book or a car. That is why a law was created that says it is wrong for anyone to steal another person's property. We must respect other people's property.

These rules apply to everyone, giving rise to the phrase that "no person is above the law." The reason that no person is above the law is because our legal system is based on a "Rule of Law." This means that the government must treat everyone in the same way under the same circumstances. The Rule of Law enables everyone to live within the rules of our legal system.

As Abraham Lincoln said in his Gettysburg Address, our system is based on the belief that our government is "of the people, by the people and for the people." It is also based on the belief and expectation that people accept and obey these laws so that they can live in freedom and enjoy the common good.

In the United States, our laws can be traced back to England and Western Europe. The ancient Greeks were governed by the Rule of Law when they first used democracy in their cities. The Romans established a code of laws for their Holy Roman Empire, an empire that lasted hundreds of years and covered much of Europe, including England. Looking back on it now, we would not consider all of their laws to be fair. Their laws treated men differently from women, and treated landowners differently from working peasants, but the basic system of laws was established and over time applied the system of laws to everyone. In the Middle Ages, after the Roman Empire had ended, the Roman system of laws continued to be taught in schools, even in places where new governments and new systems of law were developing.

(3)

In the year 1215, the English Barons forced King John to sign a document called the "Magna Carta." In this document, he agreed that even a king was subject to the Rule of Law, in effect, creating the basis for a constitutional form of government. The Magna Carta became the authority for judges in England to decide court cases that set out the Law for the people in the realm. These cases became known as the "common law." Our Constitution adopted English common law as the basis for law in the United States.

The Founding Fathers' strong belief in the Rule of Law inspired documents that continue to govern our country today, almost 250 years after they were created: The Declaration of Independence, the United States Constitution, and the Bill of Rights.

In 1841, one of our Founding Fathers and former Presidents, John Quincy Adams, successfully persuaded the United States Supreme Court to recognize the Rule of Law in the Amistad case.

This was a case in which members of an African tribe had been kidnapped and were held against their will on the schooner Amistad. They rose up and took over the ship that was later found anchored off the coast of Connecticut in Long Island Sound.

The owners of the Amistad tried to get the ship returned to them, including its cargo and the African tribesmen who originally overtook the ship. Justice Joseph Story issued the opinion for the court and ruled that the United States was a system of laws, not of men. He ruled that the Africans were free men and that they could return to their native land.

There are countries throughout the world that have rejected the Rule of Law, and instead, imposed the rule of man, typically a military dictator. In many of these countries, one person has systematically set aside the functions of government that would otherwise serve the people.

When you read that the president of a country has declared "martial law" or that the president of a country has "suspended the constitution," or that the president of a country has set aside the Supreme Court, you know that the Rule of Law has been taken away, along with the rights and freedoms of its citizens.

Throughout our history the Rule of Law has continued to be woven into our society and our legal system, although at times the process has been very slow and painful.

After the Civil War ended in 1985, the United States passed the Fourteenth Amendment that proclaimed no state could deprive any person of due process or equal protection under the law. In 1920, (55 years later) the United States passed the Nineteenth Amendment giving women the right to vote.

The Civil Rights Movement of the early 1960s pushed to make equality a reality for everyone, as Dr. Martin Luther King expressed so powerfully in his "I have a dream" speech in 1963 at the Lincoln Memorial. Soon after, Congress passed the Civil Rights Act of 1964 that represented another major milestone in guaranteeing the Rule of Law would be respected by everyone.

To live by the Rule of Law, the people of the United States have made an agreement with the government: If the people want the government to manage and enforce the rules for living safely and fairly in America, the people need to support the government by obeying these rules and by paying taxes for the services the government provides.

In his inauguration speech on January 20, 2009, President Barack Obama paid tribute to the Rule of Law and its importance to our country:

"Our Founding Fathers . . . drafted a charter to assure the Rule of Law and the rights of man, a charter expanded by the blood of generations. Those ideals still light the world, and we will not give them up for expedience's sake."

With those memorable words, the United States installed its first African American President with celebration and newfound hope that his presidency will bring positive change to our communities, our nation and our world.

(9)

The Rule of Law governs the planning of the infrastructure of the country, including the construction and maintenance of roads and bridges, public buildings, public schools, public libraries, the post office, city-electrical grid systems, public transit, and even our radio and television stations, among many others.

The Rule of Law is involved in the development of this infrastructure because government must apply basic rules of fairness that enable everyone to have equal access to public resources and services.

The way most people can see the Rule of Law at work is in the U.S. court system. The courts are required to show that the rules apply to everyone. The judges pledge to apply the laws fairly to those who appear before them. This pledge holds true even if the judge believes that the acts allegedly committed by the person before him are unacceptable conduct or are personally offensive.

In our system of justice, fellow members of the community are asked to sit as a jury to decide the guilt or innocence of the defendant. In doing so, these jurors must first take an oath that they will honestly and fairly listen to all of the evidence and then decide as a group what to believe and what not to believe. Ultimately, based on what they believe, they give a final judgment as to whether the defendant is guilty or not guilty.

The Rule of Law is especially important in how our court system applies our criminal laws to individuals charged with a crime. As a community, we decide with our Rule of Law what acts are acceptable and which acts are unacceptable. In the United States, all acts are legally acceptable except those acts that have been defined as criminal acts.

The purpose of criminal laws is to enable people to live in peace and enjoy their own rights and freedoms without harming other people. To protect everyone, communities have declared the following as crimes:

- Killing or physically injuring another person.
- Stealing property that belongs to another person.
- Breaking into the home of another person.
- Burning or destroying the property of another person.
- Selling or using illegal drugs.

These acts are criminal because communities have used the Rule of Law to conclude that these acts violate the rights and freedoms of all people. The individuals who commit these criminal acts should be punished for their conduct.

The government builds the infrastructure of streets, roads, and bridges. The government also established rules to keep people safe when driving, cycling or walking on streets, roads, and bridges.

This is why there are laws relating to our traffic system, laws such as:
- Drive on the right side of the road
- Stop at STOP signs.
- Do not drive over the speed limit.
- Park only in approved parking areas.

If we did not have traffic rules, the streets would be full of confusion and accidents. No one would feel safe driving or walking on our streets and roads.

All of these traffic rules are based on that same guiding principle, the Rule of Law. Laws are intended to help people live together safely in a way that lets them exercise their rights without jeopardizing the rights of others.

Imagine if someone could build a building however and wherever he wanted. What would happen if there were no rules for the builder to follow?

- Buildings might be built incorrectly and collapse.
- The electrical wiring might be installed unsafely and a fire could result.
- The plumbing fixtures might not connect to the trunk lines in the right way, causing flooding.
- A junkyard might be started right next to your backyard.

You do not want to live in a home like that. The Rule of Law provides the basis for regulations on constructing buildings, wiring for electricity, plumbing and laws that set up zoning districts for homes, businesses and even junkyards.

(14)

Everyone can see that the government has built a lot of roads, bridges, schools, libraries and even street lamps. Many people work for the government, including police officers, firefighters, judges, and school teachers.

But who pays for our roads and school buildings? Who pays the salaries for our police officers and our school teachers?

The government does, with money it has collected from its citizens. The money collected is the sum of all the taxes we pay.

These taxes may be applied to people's salaries (income tax), homes (real estate tax), or products purchased (sales tax). The principles of taxation are accepted by everyone because the Rule of Law requires that everyone must contribute to the government for the good of society.

Schools apply the same Rule of Law principles to the education system for our children. Every child has a right to a quality education in the United States. To do this, the community has to provide a school system that is open to all students and provide teachers for all students. In addition, they provide courses and facilities that allow each student an equal opportunity to develop his or her own intellectual skills and interests. Can you see how the Rule of Law helps you?

You expect to be treated with respect and fairness by your fellow classmates, and so do your classmates. With this mutual understanding, you go to school every day living the Rule of Law because you are honoring the rights and freedoms of every student, and so are your fellow students.

Each day you practice the Rule of Law in this way, you gain a better understanding of how to live peacefully in the community. It is important to be aware that when you exercise your rights and freedoms you must do so in a way that does not violate the rights and freedoms of others. Only then can you truly understand the saying that "no one is free unless everyone is free."

The Rule of Law also applies to every teacher in the classroom. Each teacher has an obligation to treat every student with respect and fairness and establish a set of rules for the classroom. The classroom rules tell the students what is expected of them, and how to behave.

Each student has an obligation to know, understand, and obey these rules.

The reason for the rules is to create an environment favorable for students to learn, where they are treated with respect and fairness by their teacher and fellow classmates.

Many principles of the Rule of Law also apply to living as a family. Each member of the family should be respectful of the rights and freedoms of other family members because it creates a home filled with peace and love. Most children recognize that their parents are working to enable them to learn and use their talents to the best of their abilities. At the same time, parents must realize that they have a responsibility to use their skills to help their children develop into responsible adults. The Rule of Law is at the heart of living well together in their family, their school, their community, and in their entire world.

From our Founding Fathers down to all of us, we recognize that we may never achieve an ideal society, a society in which the Rule of Law is applied appropriately to everyone in every situation. Yet, each one of us has the responsibility to try and personally pledge our support to the Rule of Law in our own country.

- No matter your race, creed, or color,
- No matter whether you are man or woman,
- No matter who your family is, or is not,
- No matter what country you come from,
- No matter whether you are rich or poor,

Join me in taking this pledge: I will treat everyone fairly and honestly. I will work to live in peace with my fellow citizens in the United States of America. This is the ideal society. This is the Rule of Law.

Now Let Us See What You Have Learned
Solve the Problem by Creating the Rules

Some students were having trouble playing basketball at recess because too many kids wanted to play. When all of the students played, they would run into each other and get hurt. Many of them did not get the opportunity to shoot the ball because there were so many kids playing. Everyone became upset. Write rules below that would help everyone to enjoy playing the game.

(21)

U. S. Presidents Who Were Lawyers

Throughout history, twenty-six of the presidents practiced law, and of that number only nine attended law school. The others became lawyers by serving first as apprentices. Write a letter to one of the presidents asking him about his life and accomplishments. Research the president's life before composing the letter so you are knowledgeable in your questions.

John Adams	James Garfield
Thomas Jefferson	Chester Arthur
James Monroe	Grover Cleveland
John Quincy Adams	Benjamin Harrison
Andrew Jackson	William McKinley *
Martin Van Buren	William Howard Taft *
John Tyler	Woodrow Wilson "
James Polk	Calvin Coolidge
Millard Fillmore	Franklin Roosevelt *
Franklin Pierce	Richard Nixon *
James Buchanan	Gerald Ford *
Abraham Lincoln	Bill Clinton *
Rutherford Hayes *	Barack Obama *

* Lawyers who attended law school vs. apprenticeship

The Rule of Law at Home

Write a paragraph describing how your parents demonstrate that they follow the Rule of Law at home.

_____
_____
_____
_____
_____
_____
_____
_____
_____
_____

Draw a picture below that shows how your parents follow the Rule of Law in your home.

The Perfect Classroom

Laws are rules that tell people what they can and cannot do. Classroom rules help teachers create a good place for you to learn. In your own words describe the perfect classroom.

_____
_____
_____
_____
_____
_____
_____
_____
_____
_____
_____
_____
_____
_____
_____
_____
_____
_____
_____
_____
_____
_____
_____
_____
_____
_____
_____

Test Your Understanding

Please read the following question and draw a picture that explains your answer: How does your teacher demonstrate that they follow the Rule of Law in your classroom? Draw a picture that shows how your teacher follows the Rule of Law in your classroom.

Do You Know?

Please read the following questions and write a short explanation for each question.

In our Justice System, laws are made to encourage good conduct. One of these laws prohibits (does not allow) crimes such as stealing property that belongs to another person. Write a statement that describes what these words mean to you.

_____
_____
_____
_____
_____

In our Traffic System, laws tell us how to drive correctly. If people do not follow these laws what might happen? Write a statement that describes what might happen if people do not follow our Traffic System laws.

_____
_____
_____
_____
_____

The government of the United States of America collects taxes (monies) from the citizens of the United States to pay for many different services. Read the section on Taxes in The Rule of Law activity book to identify some of the things they use the money for. Name 2 different ways the government spends tax monies.

_____
_____
_____
_____

Do you think this is a good way to spend the tax monies? Explain why. Name 1 way you would use the tax monies.

_____
_____
_____
_____

WORD SEARCH

Find each word in the puzzle below and circle it. Remember, words can be written backward, forward, vertical, horizontal or diagonal.

```
V K C O U R T O C G M A G N A C A R T A W J O G C
E C N E D N E P E D N I F O N O I T A R A L C E D
B O K W S P Z S G C H N A M F O E L U R A G L X C
X B C L S S T T E B W S M O D E E R F S E X A T
C E Y S E C L H C I T I Z E N S T C U D N O C I T
E Y L S C H A G E L G O W A L F O E L U R X O K I
D R I E O O N I P A S P R E S I D E N T O B A M A
U U M N R O I R S U W A L N O M M O C G R K G E E
C L A R P L M H E Q N F Q N O I T U T I T S N O C
A E F I E S I H R E S A T N E M N R E V O G J G I
T S C A U S R E H T A F G N I D N U O F I M U Z F
I M K F D T C M S T H G I R F O L L I B E Q D M F
O D S E D O C G N I D L I U B P P D Y T A Y G Z A
N S W A L J V E R U T C U R T S A R F N I G E J R
J A Q L C I V I L R I G H T S Q D G N K O O D I T
```

RULE OF LAW
OBEY RULES
MAGNA CARTA
FOUNDING FATHERS
COMMON LAW
DECLARATION OF INDEPENDENCE
CONSTITUTION
BILL OF RIGHTS
LAWS
RULE OF MAN
DUE PROCESS
EQUAL
CIVIL RIGHTS
GOVERNMENT
CITIZENS
SCHOOLS

PRESIDENT OBAMA
INFRASTRUCTURE
FAIRNESS
COURT
JUDGE
CRIMINAL
CONDUCT
TRAFFIC
TAXES
BUILDING CODES
EDUCATION
RIGHTS
FREEDOMS
RESPECT
FAMILY

(27)

FILL IN THE BLANK

Please fill in the blanks with the correct words or word phrases listed at the bottom of the page. Some words may be used twice.

1. _____ means the government must be open to everyone and treat everyone the same way under the same circumstances.

2. _____ is one of the origins for the rules for the United States of America.

3. _____, _____, and _____ are the framework for the United States society.

4. _____ proclaimed that no state should deprive/deny any person due process or equal protection of the law.

5. _____ means the construction of roads and bridges, public buildings and other systems for our country.

6. _____ System in the USA is what the citizens look to for understanding and applying the Rule of Law to all people.

7. _____ System has laws that enable people to live together in harmony and enjoy their own rights and freedoms without harming the rights and freedoms of others.

8. _____ provides the basis for having rules for constructing buildings, wiring homes and zoning laws.

9. _____ System has rules that apply to the use of streets, roads and bridges.

10. _____ are monies collected by the government from the citizens to provide services for our communities.

11. The Rule of Law for schools helps a student understand that he/she must _____ of others and not _____ the rights of others to learn.

12. Rules of Law for schools also provides the opportunity for _____ and _____ to establish a set of rules for the classroom, recess time, or study break that tells what is expected of everyone.

13. The Rule of Law for the family recognizes each family member must be _____ of the rights and freedoms of the other family members.

14. The Rule of Law for the family recognizes parents have the _____ to love and help their children grow into responsible adults AND children have the _____ to grow, learn and use their talents to the best of their abilities.

BILL OF RIGHTS	INFRINGE/HURT
BUILDING CODES	MAGNA CARTA
CONSTITUTION OF THE USA	RESPECT THE RIGHTS
COURT	RESPECTFUL
CRIMINAL	RESPONSIBILITY
DECLARATION OF INDEPENDENCE	RULE OF LAW
FOURTEENTH AMENDMENT	STUDENTS
INFRASTRUCTURE	TAXES

What Can You Do To Learn More?

What can you read to learn more about the Rule of Law?

Who can you talk to about the Rule of Law to learn more?
Family Members:

People at School:

Police, guards or court people:

Friends and neighbors:

What else can you do to learn about the Rule of Law?

Who would you like to tell about the Rule of Law? How will you tell them?